S0-ADU-709

Photographed by   BRADLEY SMITH
Edited by   MARTHA LONGENECKER
Curatorial consultant
to the exhibition   JOHN DARCY NOBLE

FIRST COLLECTIONS
Dolls and Folk Toys of the World

THE EXHIBITION, FIRST COLLECTIONS, WAS SPONSORED BY THE GERALD AND INEZ GRANT PARKER FOUNDATION

A MINGEI INTERNATIONAL MUSEUM EXHIBITION DOCUMENTARY PUBLICATION

MADE POSSIBLE BY THE SEYMOUR E. CLONICK MEMORIAL FUND AND SYDNEY MARTIN ROTH

THE MUSEUM GRATEFULLY THANKS THE DIRECTOR'S CIRCLE, THE EXHIBITION SPONSORS AND ALL WHO
LENT FROM THEIR COLLECTIONS AND CONTRIBUTED TO THE CREATION AND PRESENTATION OF *FIRST*
COLLECTIONS AND THIS LIBRARY RECORD OF SOME OF OUR WORLD'S MOST CHARMING ART TREASURES

Library of Congress Catalog No. 87-62951
Published by Mingei International
Museum of World Folk Art

University Towne Centre, 4405 La Jolla Village Drive
(mailing address: P. O. Box 553, La Jolla, CA 92038)

Copyright © 1987 U.S.A.
by Mingei International Museum

All rights reserved.

ISBN #0-914155-05-9

MINGEI INTERNATIONAL MUSEUM IS A FULLY ACCREDITED MEMBER OF THE AMERICAN ASSOCIATION OF MUSEUM

CONTENTS

COVER — LENCI DOLLS—ITALY (early 20th C.)
        SCHOENHUT TOY—Painted wood, jointed legs and head. 6″ tall—U.S.A. (1913)
BELOW — JACK IN A BOX TOY—Spring toy in a McGinty's watch case.
        2″ tall.—GERMANY (1850)
FOLLOWING PAGES — WOODEN DOG ROLL TOY—Moveable head, ears and tail,
        2′ long.—FRANCE (19th C.)

It is not the unique individual who speaks through dolls and toys, but the anonymous collective mind with millennia of traditional knowledge. The form of expression, ranging from realism to abstraction, simplicity to fantasy, is as modern as it is timeless.

Dolls and toys have many layers of meaning. Even when their significance is lost to the intellect, their impact may still be felt.

This rich tradition is now dying out. It is true that children will always need toys, but if the flying horse gives way to the mechanical hen that lays plastic eggs, a great heritage will be lost. We cannot prevent that by mere sentiment; the whole question is bound up with the art of living of an entire community. Revival depends on a change of values, a de-vulgarization of life and a return to collective wholeness.

AJIT MOOKERJEE

CARVED PAINTED WOOD PULL TOY
18" tall.
GERMANY   19th C.
Collection of anonymous lender

PREFACE *by Martha Longenecker, Director*

The seeing and handling of dolls and toys is one of a person's first and most intimate contacts with a work of art—a beautiful and tactile object! Appealing in line, form and color, these delightful and imaginative *FIRST COLLECTIONS* are enhanced by their manipulation in play, stimulating a child's creative powers. It is said, "Play is the work of a child, and toys are his tools."

Dolls and toys are often made for a particular child by family members or friends—the intensity of their love for the child heightening the expressive quality and appeal of the creation. Among these dolls and folk toys are to be discovered the pure expressions of human beings at their best.

Almost any material can be used for the making of dolls and toys—straw and other natural fibers, bits of string, scraps of wood, cloth, paper, leather, wire and metal, as well as common clay. The challenge of working with these materials is the same as in the creation of any art object, requiring imagination, inventiveness, aesthetic sensitivity and skill.

Dolls and toys, in some magical way, awaken in us a quality of wonder. Enchanting and *amusing* playthings, they seem to reflect the realm of the Muses—that world in which things of daily life correspond to the eternal, transcendent world which one can only refer to obliquely through suggestion or intimation.

DOLLS AND TOYS — OUR FIRST LOVES
by John Darcy Noble

Curator Emeritus of Dolls and Toys at The Museum of the City of New York

On Mount Olympus, the Gods of classical antiquity passed their days in play. It was an arduous task indeed to secure their interest in the dull and adult concerns of mortals. Play was their godly occupation.

Throughout the animal kingdom, it is the more highly evolved creatures who delight in play, often flinging themselves, as do otters and dolphins, into the physical expression of their joie de vivre. Only Man, with his anxieties and his self-conciousness, rejects play as childishness, relegating it to his children, and expressing this most innocent and holy of urges only in the cupidity of cardgames, or the evasion of spectator sports.

There are, of course, exceptions. Primitive races, untouched by the dubious involvements of civilization, play happily, while among the cultured ones, it is the highly evolved artist, amongst others, who devotes himself, with religious fervor and single-mindedness, to a lifetime of play.

WOODEN JOINTED DOLL *previous page*
This rare and perhaps unique doll with its expressive and beautiful face has carved red shoes of the style worn by aristocrats. 20″ tall.
NORTHERN EUROPE (FLEMISH)   18th C.

WOODEN DOLL
18″ tall.

ENGLAND   18th C.

The urge to collect is not divine, but it is widespread among men. A few animals, apes and magpies and even some wayward cats, collect the bright and shining objects that touch their fancy. The urge to collect can be seen to have, at least, a mystical quality, if not a godly one, being, as Vivien Greene* has so aptly quoted "inspired by a curiosity that helps to defeat the profound sadness of life."

Possessiveness, a less worthy factor, cannot be ignored in these lofty musings, but it becomes less base when we realize that by possessing the intriguing object, we hope to encompass it — to take it to ourselves.

This helps us to understand our little children, as they make their first collections, stepping out on unsteady legs into the great, sunlit world with wonder in their eyes, picking up, for the first time, the convoluted shells from the beach, the rounded pebbles from the stream and the transient flowers, the bright berries and shining, magical feathers from the woodland.

Such collections can influence profoundly our development. Henry Moore, the English sculptor, cherished shelvesful of twisted roots, bones and worn eroded stones, to which he turned again and again for refreshment and inspiration. *continued on page 20*

*Mrs. Graham Greene is the renowned collector, author, and authority on dolls' houses.

WOODEN DOLL

Exceptionally rare in her baby doll-clothes. 20″ tall.

ENGLAND   18th C.

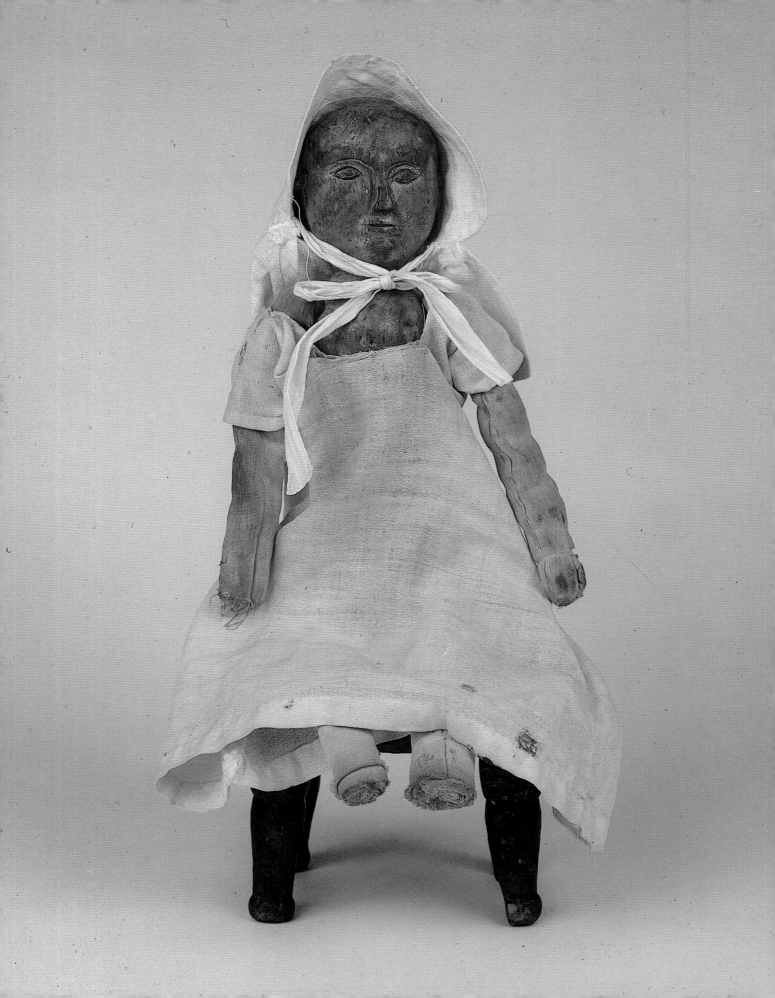

WOODEN DOLL *previous pages*

12"tall.

U.S.A.   18th C.

Collection of anonymous lender

AMISH CLOTH DOLL

(on right)

14" tall.

U.S.A.   1850

CLOTH DOLL

Made over a potato masher. 11" tall.

U.S.A.   1850

Collection of anonymous lender

EARLY PRIMITIVE "DOLL"

What appears to be a child's doll is in fact a church figure of the Christ
Child in Majesty, its hands positioned to hold orb and sceptre, its head
drilled to support crown and halo. Its descent to the nursery remains
a mystery.

Painted wood, jointed arms, 22" tall.

SPAIN   late 16th or early 17th C.

Collection of Mingei International

The toys that children collect are less personal, since they mostly have no part in the choosing of them. Small children are unselective, and will play as happily with a knotted handkerchief as with an expensive, realistic doll — and often, to the chagrin of their parents, prefer the former. But children's toys do tell us a great deal about those parents, who chose the toys, remembering surely their own lost childhood.

In reviewing the playthings of our past in conjunction with those of other cultures, one is struck, not by the differences of race and climate, although these are demonstrated in fascinating ways, but rather by the similarities, by the expressions of the urge to play that are common, we find, to all mankind.

A doll, a doll's house, a toy horse, a cart on wheels, a ball, a toy bird, a toy fish; these are but a few of the many basic toys to be found in the first collections of people from all over the world, objects that are profound symbols, we realize at last, not just of the child's curiosity about life, but of the man's mystical relationship to life itself, in all its marvelous manifestations.

ADAM AND EVE IN PARADISE

German flat lead toy. The first in a long line of such metal toys, these "flats" first appeared in Germany in the late 18th century. They covered a bewildering spectrum of human activities before they settled into the soldiery, farmyards and menageries of the 19th century. This "Paradise" with its dignified Adam and Eve and its range of concerned, apprehensive animals, is from the 1830's.

GERMANY   c. 1830

Collection of John Darcy Noble

Again, to quote the wise Vivien Greene, "A pig is charming, and so is a toy pig; anyone would want to play with either." A bird is a bird and a fish is a fish. Their existences are parallel to ours, yet forever separate. We can never understand them, however much we kill them — or perhaps we kill them because we cannot understand them, and here our children have the better of us, for at least they try. They look at birds and fish with wonder, and, as they play with them by proxy, perhaps get closer to the truth of them than all our dissecting scientists.

The doll can be the closest of companions, the sharer of infant joys and sorrows, or it can personify the dream of the grown-up person the child would wish to be, just as the dolls' house is security made tangible. In the same way, the toy birds and fishes are surrogates for those marvels of nature, while the horse is, of course, the ancient symbol of adventure, of quest, of the yearning for all that is noble in our nature.

EARLY GREINER DOLL

Unmarked. 25½″ tall.

With French mechanical toy of cat on tricycle and German pull toy

GERMANY   1845

Collection of anonymous lender

We learn more from the artifacts of a culture, long ago or far away, than from all the discussions and theories of the learned. This is the value and the enduring fascination of our museums. And of all the artifacts that these institutions enshrine, those made for children's play are the most vivid, evoking the direct response, lifting the heart with delight, or inducing the most subtle of melancholies.

There are indeed, profound lessons to be learned as we look at these toys, these fragile and touching evidences of the wonder of childhood. If we learn to open our hearts, as well as our minds, if we can allow our instincts towards play their freedom as we survey these dolls, these toy horses and toy houses, and birds and fishes, then we are paving the way towards a better understanding of our fellow men, and of our universal humanity. And if we do this, we will find ourselves, unexpectedly, a little closer to the Gods.

PULL TOY

Wood and wool. 7″ tall.

GERMANY   19th C.

Collection of anonymous lender

CAT ON TRICYCLE   *previous pages*

Mechanical toy.

Painted wood, paper and wire, 14″ tall.

FRANCE   c. 1890

Collection of anonymous lender

PEDDLER DOLL

Part of a family group of three. 15″ tall.

GERMANY   c. 1830

Collection of John Darcy Noble

WAX DOLL

20″ tall.

ENGLAND   1850

Collection of Mingei International

JOEL ELLIS DOLL

Rock maple with mortise and tenon joints, rigid head,
metal hands and feet. Lathe-turned, with head pressed
under steam pressure and hand-painted. 15½″ tall.

U.S.A.   1872

MOTSCHMANN DOLL

6″ tall.

GERMANY   c. 1870

Collection of anonymous lender

NOAH'S ARK   *following pages*

Carved painted wood. 17″ tall.

GERMANY   1840

Collection of anonymous lender

DOLLS AND TOYS EVERYWHERE
by Bradley Smith

When the world was fresh and new there were few people and animals around. Men and women had each other and their children to keep them from being lonesome and the animals had each other. But the children, the poor lonely things, had nothing but mothers and fathers who lived in their own "grownup" world; and their younger or older sisters and brothers who were terrible. So, out of an infinite wisdom the great spirit caused dolls to be!

In ancient American Indian life, dolls made for the children were created in forms and shapes of the many spirits that the Zuni, Hopi and Navajo people believed lived under the waters and beneath the earth. There were many such spirits — over two hundred (and there still are). They took care of the pure waters, the fertile earth, thunder and rain and lightning, and even thoughts and ideas. And so, from these dolls, which were called Kachinas (the Indian word of the gods), the children learned about life and the magical world of spirits.

In the modern world, the *New International Webster's Dictionary* records that "a doll is a small scale figure of a human being as of a baby, used as a child's plaything." But all children know better! What then is a doll?

WELLINGTON DOLL

Painted cloth. 25″ tall.

U.S.A.   1883

Collection of anonymous lender

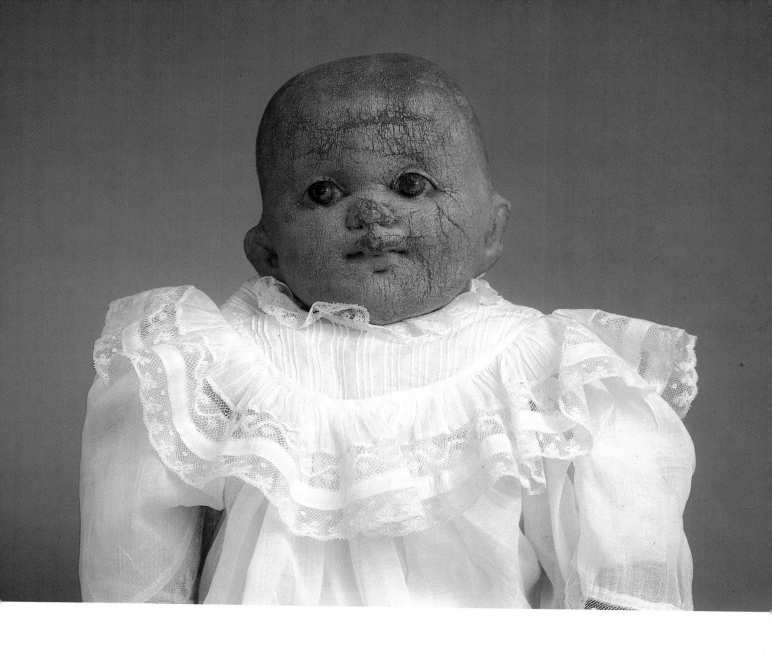

A doll is a little person with its own life, a life created by the love, care and affection of its owner. The doll becomes a part of the special world (outside the grownup world) of children. Dolls absorb the human warmth and the special reality of the child's world.

Like the beautiful statue, in Greek mythology, of Galatea, who lived because of the love of its sculptor creator, Pygmalion, the doll lives because of the love of its friend, confidant, caretaker owner. Yet a doll does not imitate its owner. Within its own environment the doll develops its distinctive personality. And within the mind and heart of the child the doll lives forever, although its image fades away as its owner leaves childhood and crosses over to become a grownup.

A toy is something else, for while a toy may be enjoyed and treasured, it leads a rough life. It gets less loving care, yet it is a joyous extension of a child's spirit of play. Toys are pulled, pushed, ridden, kicked and moved in myriad patterns. Unlike the doll, it never sleeps nor does it need as much affection. Yet it too has a life of its own and is never completely forgotten.

So hooray! and wow! and bang! and go to sleep dolly — wake up! dolls and toys. May you ever be with us.

CARTON BABY

Painted papier-mache, 20″ tall.

FRANCE   1910

Collection of anonymous lender

HOBBY HORSE   *previous page*

Carved wood. 6′ x 5′.

EARLY AMERICAN

Collection of Frank Papworth

BOY DOLL

Wood head and arms, cloth body. 22″ tall.

AMERICAN   19th C.

Collection of anonymous lender

JOINTED DOLL

Wax over papier-mache head, jointed composition body. 32" tall.

GERMANY   early 20th C.

Collection of anonymous lender

PAINTED REDWOOD DOLL HOUSE

With removeable front   40″ tall.

CALIFORNIA, U.S.A.   c. 1890

Collection of anonymous lender

ROCKING HORSE   *following pages*

Painted wood, 5″ tall.

GERMANY   1860

Collection of anonymous lender

JACK-IN-THE-BOX

Bisque head, wood arms. In painted wood box. 8″ long.

GERMANY   1890

Collection of anonymous lender

DOLLS WITH CHINA PAINTED HEADS

16″ and 11″ tall.

GERMANY   late 19th C.

52   Collection of Mingei International

TETE JUMEAU

Musical automated wind-up dolls. Painted bisque head
and arms, real hair. 24″ tall.

FRANCE   c. 1880

54   Collection of Mingei International

JUMEAU BÉBÉ

Unmarked. 9″ tall.

PARIS BÉBÉ

11 ″ tall.

Bisque-head dolls, jointed composition bodies.

FRANCE   1880

56   Collection of anonymous lender

LITTLE LIZZIE

A marked French Jumeau doll with a German, Simon and Halbig replacement head. This winsome little person achieved considerable fame in England in the 1950's, when a classic rag doll was named after her.

Bisque head, jointed composition body. 15″ tall.

FRANCE   1894

Collection of John Darcy Noble

BADEKINDER OR BATHING DOLL

These toys were made in a range of sizes, from tiny miniatures one inch long, to the great, heavy creature depicted here, which is all of 16 inches tall. These toys were first made in the 1860's, and were consistently popular for the next thirty years.

Glazed china.

GERMANY   1880

Collection of John Darcy Noble

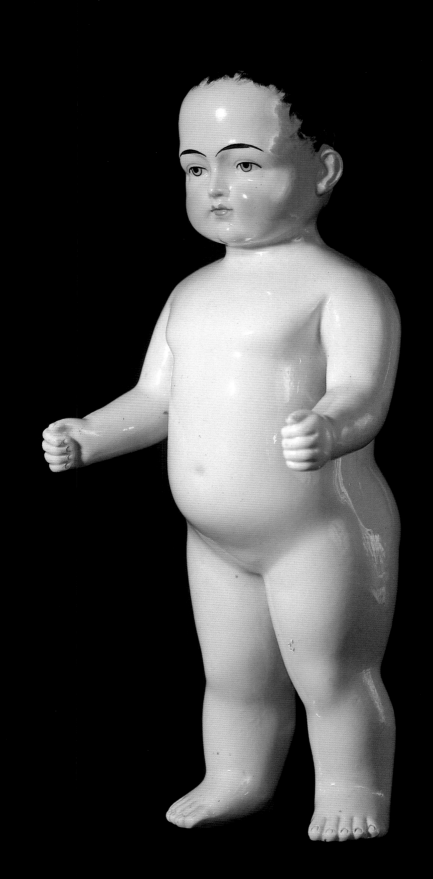

LENCI DOLLS

Painted felt faces. 17″ tall.

ITALY   early 20th C.

Collection of Mingei International

MARGUERITE "BONNET" DOLLS

At the end of a long line of beautiful bisque dolls, produced over a span of sixty years, these frivolous creatures appeared in the early 1900's as a last burst of creativity. Comparatively crude in both material and execution, they have a bravura charm and sugary texture which is both surprising and pleasing. The group here, wearing flowers and insects as head dresses, were known as "Marguerites."

Bisque head, arms and feet. Cloth body.

GERMANY   1900

Collection of John Darcy Noble

PULL TOY

Painted papier-mache with wire springs and wheels.
Leather reins. 13″ tall.

FRANCE   c.1850

66   Collection of anonymous lender

BOY ON TRICYCLE

Mechanical toy.
Wood, cloth and metal. 9″ tall.

U.S.A.   1860

68   Collection of anonoymous lender

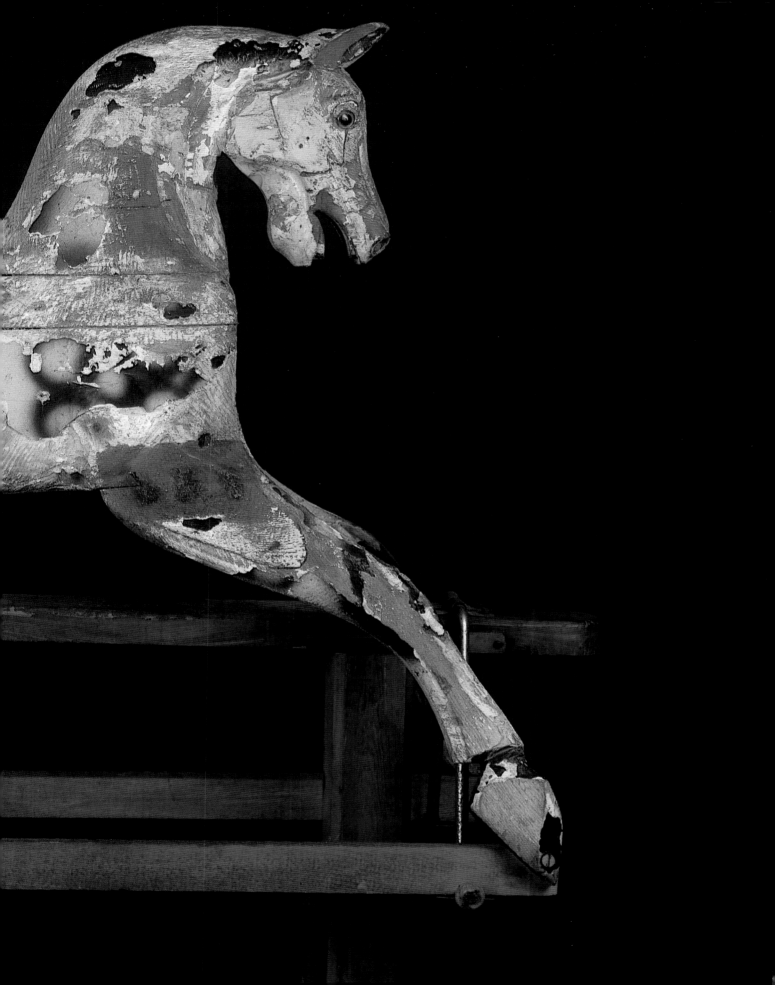

GLIDER HORSE *previous pages*

Carved painted wood. 41" tall.

SCOTLAND   early 20th C.

Collection of anonymous lender

ALI GROOZE MECHANICAL ROLL TOY *following page*

Wood, paper and wire. 16" tall.

EGYPT   1978

Collection of The Children's Museum, Indianapolis, Indiana

CYMBAL PLAYING DOLLS

Cymbals clang together when doll is squeezed. Wood
stick body with painted clay head, painted paper clothes.
8" tall.

EGYPT   20th C.

Collection of Mingei International

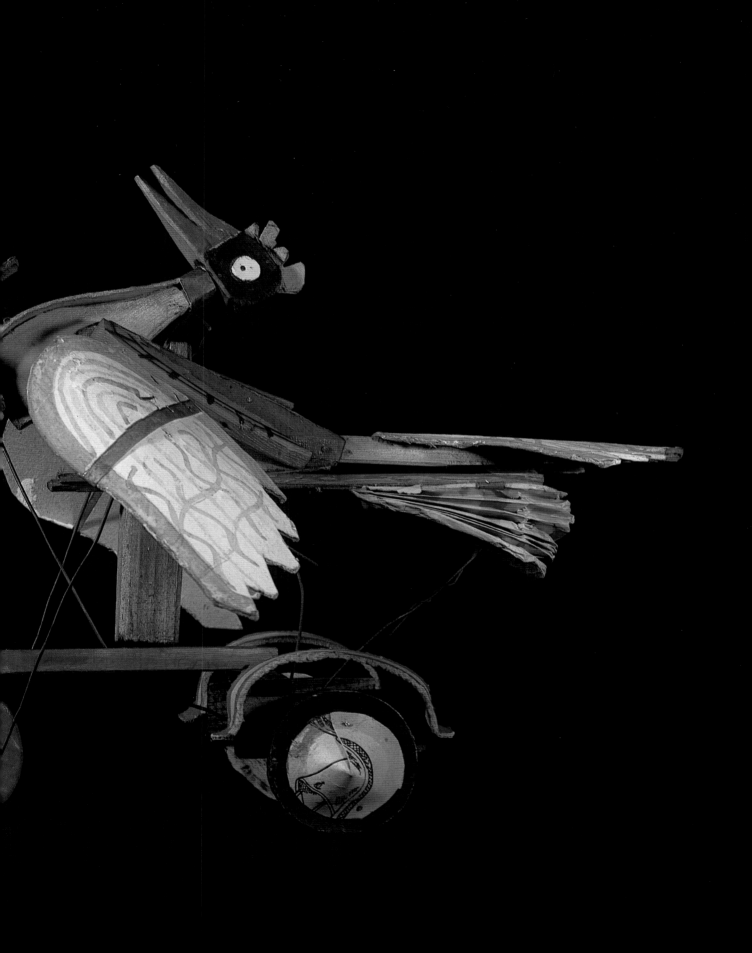

DOLLS AND TOYS OF INDIA
by Ajit Mookerjee

"The link between ritual and play is intimate. A woman makes an image of Sasthi, a household deity, and at the same time explains the Vrata-story to the children sitting around her, so that when they get the same image as a thing to play with, the theme persists in their minds. The toy to them becomes a symbol of something they know, not what they merely see, thus fulfilling their inner needs and desires. Likewise, toy animals also perform a double role, retaining all the qualities of a type the earliest specimens of which have been found at Harappa, Mohenjo-daro and other chalcolithic sites...

However interesting the front of most of the figurines may be, the back is always simple and unimpressive. The Red Indians keep the back of their toys comparatively bare in the belief that this will help their children live long. A similar belief may have existed in India too, but no wholly satisfactory explanation is available why our dolls and toys are invariably meant to be looked at from the front only...

CARVED WOODEN DOLLS

Tallest 14".

INDIA   19th C.

Collection of anonymous lender

Of material used besides clay in toy-making, wood is the most common. Dolls are also made from pith, papier-mache, cow-dung, bronze, rags and vegetable fibres—the use of the last two being practically extinct. The makers of wood, pith and bronze toys are guild artists, known as sutradhara (carpenter), malakara (garland maker), and karmakara (metal worker), and they are usually menfolk, whereas in the potter's (kumbhakara) family women and children generally play an important role.

Each material presents its own problems of form and treatment; wood and pith works, for instance, have to be angular, whereas a bronze doll has much greater plastic tension...

Indian dolls and toys sometimes open up a world which knows no frontiers. They show striking affinities with certain types found in Egypt, in Crete, and even in centres of the Maya civilization. Flinders Petri points out that in the workmen's quarters at Memphis there are Indian-type terracottas of women and of the seated Kuvera. D.H. Gordon says that a linking of all the terracottas of the Hellenistic period from the Eastern Mediterranean to Bengal is necessary...

CARVED PAINTED WOOD DOLLS

The backs are flat and undecorated. 7″ tall.

INDIA   20th C.

Collection of Mingei International

Sometimes the link between a particular doll and a story, which is lost in this country, may be traced abroad where our folk tales travelled in very ancient times. In Japan, Daruma (Dharma) dolls are dedicated to Yakusi, the Buddhist God of Medicine and the Guruma type has something in common with an ancient Japanese toy known as Buriburi. The Guruma toy traces its origin to a very old and celebrated legend of Umi-sati and Yama-sati.

That the Indian tradition has survived innumerable vicissitudes through the ages is due to the fact that the social organization was based on the village community, in the corporate life of which artists and craftsmen played their assigned roles. The potter, for instance, was given plots of land or fixed quantities of grain at harvest time by village people in exchange for which he supplied them their requirements, dolls and toys included. The malakara functioned in the same way. The system meant security, without which the artists and artisans could not have developed their crafts in close touch with tradition. Under such conditions, the craftsman worked out age-old forms, and countless recapitulations resulted in a state of mind in which he could reproduce the most abstract without any conscious effort or distortion. Even where he made

MINIATURE DOLLS
Carved painted wood. 3″ tall.
ANDHRA PRADESH (?), INDIA   20th C.
80   Collection of Mingei International

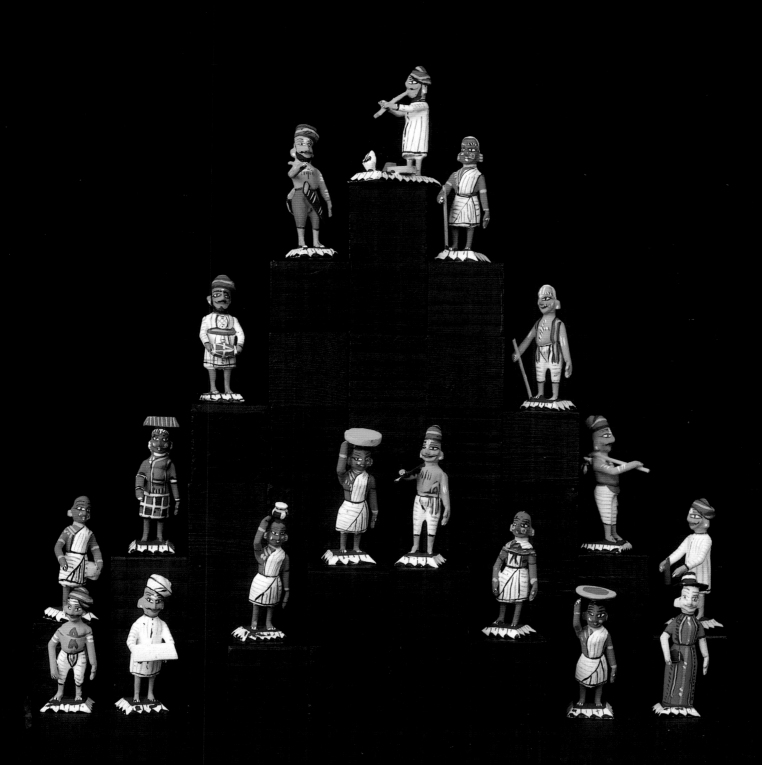

a significant change, he was perhaps unaware of it. He could introduce new patterns, give the old a new look, but the possibilities of a radical assertion of his individuality in the modern sense were very much limited because of the total impact of a social and religious structure extending from the joint family to the panchayat.

Another important factor for the continuity of tradition was mythology and folk-tales, always a source of stimulation to the rural artist. Their dramatic intensity is felt most in the dolls and toys still made by the few tribes that have survived in more or less inaccessible areas. In these, art and magic are almost inseparable. A village potter can make a tiger without any story element, but a tribal tiger must have some association with a legend and an element of mantra and, therefore, a form and fantasy of its own.

The Adivasis, though scattered and isolated, maintain a pattern of abstract art which is more or less similar. They still hold clues to hidden rituals, which include the sound-values of many images, akin to the Tantric Vija-mantras, whose meaning can help further study of Indian iconography.

CARVED PAINTED WOOD DOLL

19″ tall.

RAJASTHAN, INDIA   late 19th — early 20th C.

Collection of anonymous lender

With the impact of the industrial revolution and new forms of economy, disintegration of the old Indian system began and the village craftsman was dissociated from the rest of the community. He lost his grip over social reality and also some important secrets of the ancient technique. Decadence of content and form is evident, but even now the force of tradition neutralizes the shortcomings to a minimum, making the contemporary product something that is always tolerable. However, where commercialization dominates, the result is unfortunate.

A systematic study of Indian dolls and toys can be a fascinating incursion into our cultural patterns, revealing historical and psychological trends of great importance. In fact, folk toys are in a way the autobiography of the Indian people."

From Folk Toys of India. Calcutta & New Delhi: Oxford Book & Stationery Co. Courtesy of Ajit Mookerjee

CLAY TOY

7" tall.

ASSAM, INDIA   20th C.

Collection of Mingei International

BRONZE TOY

Lost wax method, 5″ tall.

BRONZE LION TOY

Lost wax method, 7″ tall.

BASTAR, INDIA 20th C.

Collection of anonymous lender

BRIDAL COUPLE

Painted faces, fabric clothing embellished with metallic papers. 17″ tall.

MADHYA PRADESH, INDIA   20th C.

88   Collection of Mingei International

BRIDAL COUPLE

Painted papier-mache head & hands. Silk
embroidered garments. 11″ tall.

CHINA   1920

Collection of Mingei International

STRING PUPPET

Carved painted wood, sisal tail and mane, yarn and
paper trappings, 20″ long.

BURMA   20th C.

92   Collection of Mingei International

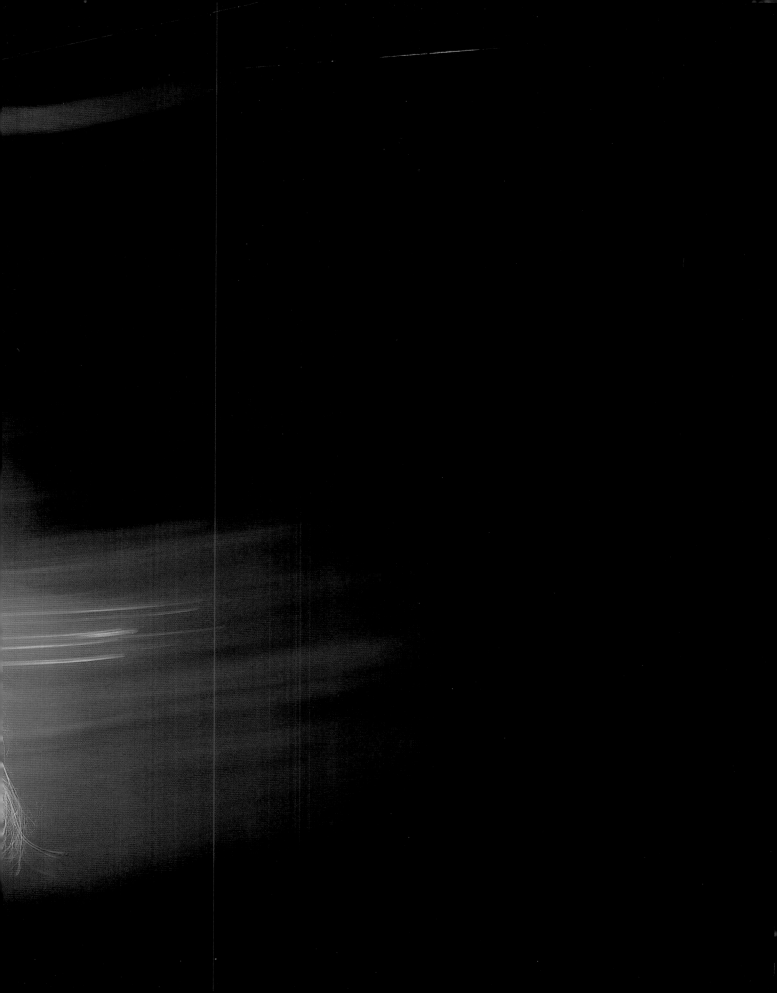

CARVED PAINTED WOOD DOLL

Jointed, 5″ tall.

BURMA   20th C.

Collection of Mingei International

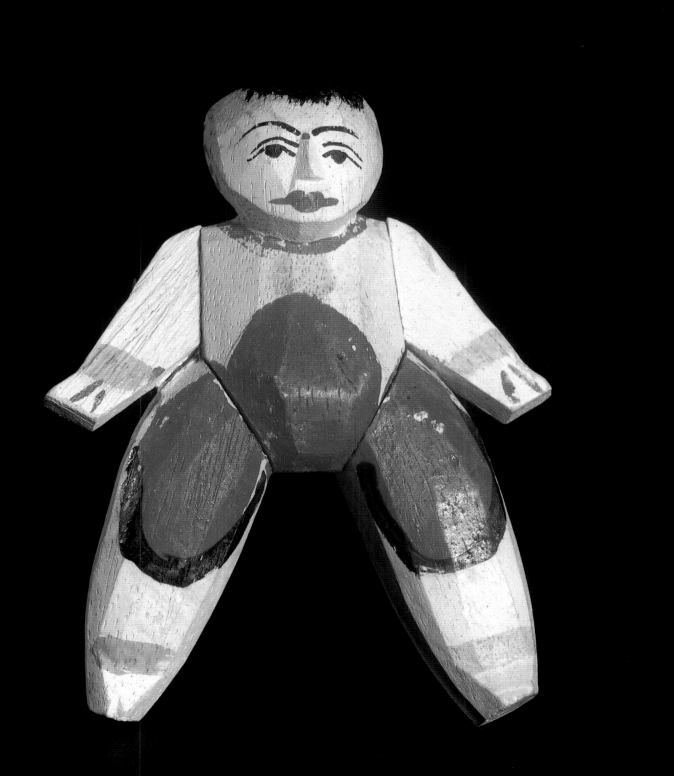

ZUNI KACHINA DOLLS

Carved painted cottonwood. Tallest 9″.

NATIVE AMERICAN   20th C.

Collection of Mingei International

LEATHER AND CLOTH DOLL
With handwoven wool clothing, 17″ tall.
NATIVE AMERICAN, HOPI   c. 1910

100   Collection of Mingei International

PLAINS INDIAN DOLLS

Beaded leather, 13" tall.

NATIVE AMERICAN   20th C.

Collection of The Children's Museum, Indianapolis, Indiana

INUIT DOLL

Fur with leather applique, 19″ tall.

NATIVE AMERICAN   20th C.

104   Collection of The Children's Museum, Indianapolis, Indiana

JAPANESE GAMES AND TOYS

In the beginning of all people's cultural development, they live as one with the world. A stone is as much alive as a man is, as much a friend or enemy as is a tree. A stone that is shaped like a turtle is assumed to once have been a turtle; because turtles, stones, trees, man, the elements—they are all one, of the same cosmic heartbeat.

Comes a time when people wish to explain what they experience. Then it is that they create "gods" — those other-worldly forces which cause, which have personalities, and which are to be appeased or cajoled (depending upon what they cause). Now the turtle became a stone because a god changed it into stone. If that happened, there must have been a reason. And myths, legends and traditions are born.

Some people eventually substitute the latter explanations for the original feeling of oneness with the world. Others, of whom only a few are left on earth, have not made any substitutions at all.

The Japanese are one of the amazing handful of peoples who have managed to do both.

KOKESHI DOLLS

Lathe-turned, painted wood, 20″ tall and under.

TOHOKU, JAPAN   20th C.

Collection of Mingei International

They know a god did not turn a turtle into a stone—that the stone has always been a stone which happened to be shaped like a turtle. Yet they love the turtle it used to be.

All the traditional games and toys of Japan are expressions of this harmonious dichotomy to greater or lesser degrees. Even though some are available nowadays in modern materials—plastics, styrofoam, etc.—everyone knows what they used to be made of and why. And many are used today specifically and solely as amulets.

Most folk toys are related to shrines because the toys themselves were originally the result of a story that related to a shrine. Either the story happened in or near a shrine, or the deity involved in the story is the same as the one to whom a shrine is dedicated. Through the centuries, the practice developed and prevailed of making a donation to the shrine and receiving the "toy" in thanks; or making the donation *in order* to receive the amulet, depending on how desperate a person felt at the moment. To this day, "amulet-toys" which have a shrine-related tradition are available for purchase

BENTA DOLL (BENTA-NINGYO)

Hand-carved painted paulownia wood. Limbs are attached to the body with red strips of cotton — originated from a Korean clay doll, 14″ tall.

JAPAN 20th C.

Collection of Mingei International

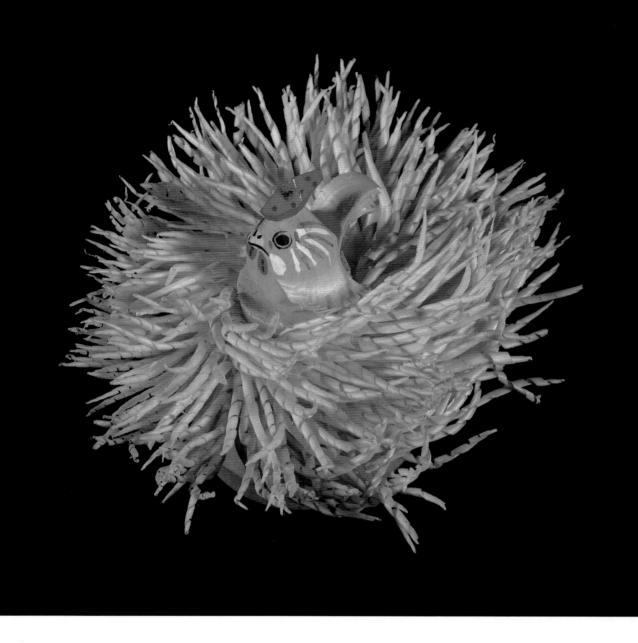

SASANO CARVING

Chicken in the nest, 4″ tall.

Falcon, 18″ tall.

Carved from a single block of walnut or other hardwood
following a 1,000-year-old tradition resembling methods
used by the aboriginal Ainu.

YONEZAWA, YAMAGATA PREFECTURE,
JAPAN   20th C.

Collection of Mingei International

(donation) at that shrine, whether it be in the middle of a big city or in the country.

Other "amulet-toys," used to protect, provide, persuade, etc., were not related to specific shrines, since they were not the products of stories. They were invented by craftsmen out of the living conditions of the times, and were sold in shops. For example, before the development of medical sciences, various amulets were created to ward off illnesses or to cure existing ones. These types of charms are still available in shops; and nowadays shrine-related charms can also be purchased in shops.

The forms and themes of Japanese folk toys are rich in variety, most being representational with few abstract designs.

Almost all of the animals, birds, fish and insects indigenous to Japan are accounted for, simply because through the ages the Japanese people have lived in close relationships with these creatures. Dolls represent deities, historical figures, legendary figures and ordinary men, women and children. In both categories, an occasional import is found—like a

PAINTED WOODEN HORSE TOY

5″ long.

HIROSAKI, AOMORI PREFECTURE,
JAPAN   19th C.

Gift of Keisuke Serizawa

Collection of Mingei International

tiger—which is not native to the country but which has captured the imagination of the people.

The materials originally used for these folk toys were always those immediately available in the region. A papier-mache toy immediately suggests its "city" origin: during the Edo period, a sheet of paper was so precious that people saved every piece they could find to use again for something else. Papier-mache toys came only from towns where Daimyo (feudal lords) lived. Being educated, the Daimyo corresponded on paper, and every scrap they threw away was snatched up by the townspeople and used by the craftsmen. Since paper was nonexistent in farming villages, their toys were made in local natural materials: wood, clay, grasses and bamboo. In their spare time, carpenters would fashion wooden toys for their children out of leftover wood, and tile bakers made clay toys.

The colors, too, related to the region. Since Japan has many climates, some toys originated in balmy areas; their colors are delicate, pale, quiet. Toys from more extreme climates are in vivid, contrasting hues.

WHEELED WOODEN TOY
Pheasant horse, 7″ long.
SHIMIZU, KYUSHU ISLAND, JAPAN
late 19th — early 20th C.

Collection of Mingei International

One of the most interesting aspects of Japan's games and toys is their incredible number and variety. Historically, this is a result of political conditions. For many centuries Japanese governments not only isolated the country from communication with the rest of the world, but also severely restricted travel within the country for political reasons. This policy, plus a basic lack of adequate transportation facilities, resulted in regional and even communal isolation. Each area, then, created its own toys, games and amulets, which became traditional to the community or region. Hence, today we see thousands of different traditional toys and games throughout Japan.

In all societies, toys as playthings or as talismans have a definite hierarchical structure, in accordance with societal structures. In Japan, the aristocracy—the Emperor, court attendants and feudal lords—enjoyed many games, including Go and *Karuta*, playing cards. Samurai—the warrior class, second in hierarchy—enjoyed *Shogi*. In feudal Japan, the lower hierarchical ranks of society were occupied by the farmer, the craftsman and the merchant, in that order. It was in these groups that toys as amulets were indulged in most. These people lived closer to nature and had far

WHEELED WOODEN TOY

25″ long.

KYUSHU, JAPAN   20th C.

Collection of Mingei International

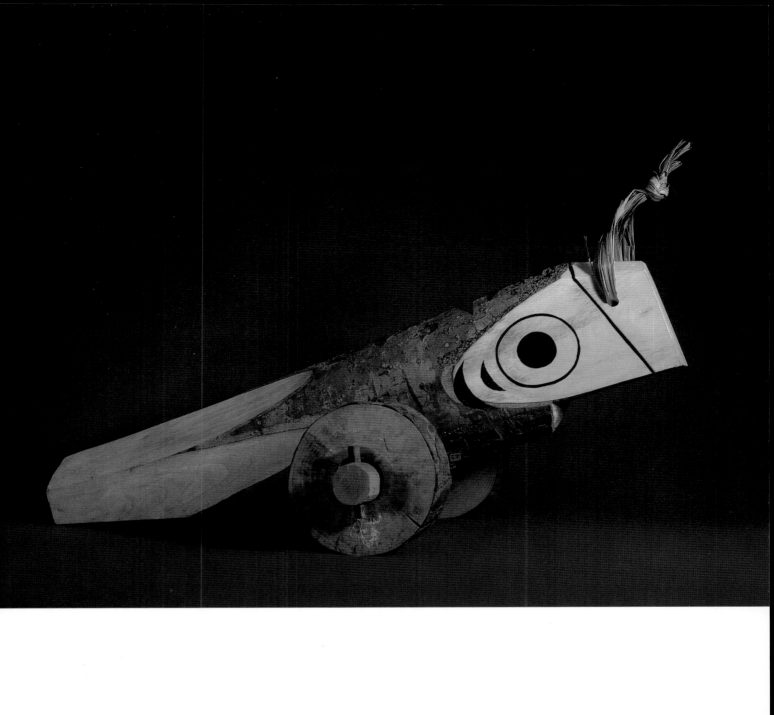

more "worries" in their daily lives than had the aristocracy or the samurai. From these people, then, Japan has inherited her treasure of talismans for good business, good weather, good friendships, good health, and so on.

Westerners who are introduced to the folk toys of Japan have often become enamoured of their beauty and their "powers." It is true that the charms will "work" for anyone, whether Japanese or not, because, of course, the gods exist for all who are open to them. One warning though: If you wish to step inside this world— or, rather, step *out* into this world—your heart must be pure. You too must love the turtle who became a stone.

From Japanese Games and Toys, Hitachi Ltd.
Courtesy of the editor, Tsune Sesoko

TIGER OF SHINNO SHRINE (SHINNO-NO-TORA)

Painted papier-mache tiger. Bobbing head, 5″ long.

During the annual November festival of the Shinno shrine, favored by pharmacists, the toy tiger is attached to a twig of bamboo grass and sold to worshippers as a charm against epidemics.

RED COW OR OX (ADABEKO)

Painted papier-mache, 7″ long.

Used as a charm against smallpox, first made 100 years ago as a child's toy.

FUKUSHIMA, JAPAN,   1979

Collection of Mingei International

SERVANT DOLL (HOKO-SAN)

Many customs have developed around the *yomeiri*—the Japanese bride's entry into her husband's home. In the northern area of the island of Shikoku, an important part of the bride's luggage used to be a set of dolls, which were intended as gifts for the children in the husband's family. The more dolls a girl brought, the better was the impression she made. These were humble clay or papier-mache figures, but they showed whether a girl was thoughtful enough to select the most appropriate good luck charms.

No *yomeiri* collection would be complete without *Hoko-San*, the faithful servant. A long time ago, according to legend, there lived a little girl named Omaki. Her family was poor, so she was sent out to become a servant in the mansion of a local samurai. She served the daughter of the house, who became afflicted with an incurable disease. Omaki, feeling sorry for the maiden, drew the disease into her own body to save the samurai's daughter. Ever since, when a village child comes down with the chicken pox, the little doll *Hoko-San* is placed in bed with the patient for one night and the following morning is set adrift on a river to take away the child's sickness.

Painted papier-mache, 6″ tall.

SHIKOKU, JAPAN   20th C.

Collection of Mingei International

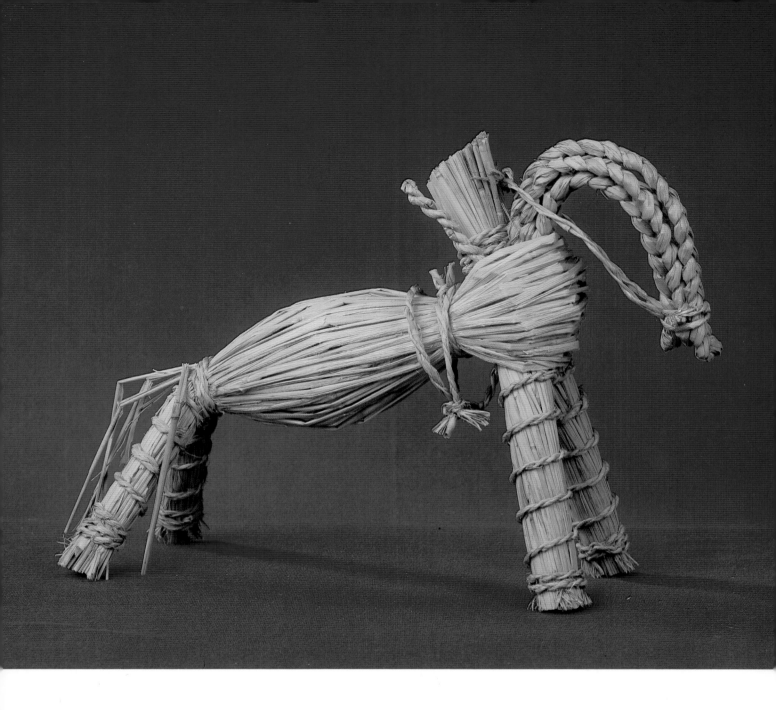

NATURAL FIBER HORSE
7″ tall.

NATURAL FIBER HORSE
Head and neck are woven in braids. 9″ tall.

JAPAN   20th C.

Collection of Mingei International

NATURAL FIBER ELEPHANTS

Big elephant: CHINA   7″ tall.

Little elephant: AFRICA   4″ tall.

NATURAL FIBER DONKEY

Painted corn husk. 13″ tall.

MEXICO   20th C.

124   Collection of James Steele Smith

TRIBAL DOLL

Terra Cotta clay.

Simple expressive clay dolls have been made for millenia throughout the world. They continue to be created as a most basic toy especially in areas where there are few materials other than the clay of the earth. While the organic materials disintegrate with time, the inorganic fired clay dolls endure.

INDIA   1980

PRE-COLUMBIAN CLAY DOLL

7″ tall.

MEXICO

Collection of anonymous lender

PAINTED CLAY BULL

By Rosendo Rodriguez. 17″ tall.

MEXICO   c. 1980

128   Collection of Mingei International

PAINTED PAPIER-MACHE DOLLS

10″ tall.

MEXICO   20th C.

Collection of Mingei International

KANGAROO

By Manuel Jimenez
Carved wood, analine dyed. 12″ tall.

MEXICO   20th C.

Collection of James Steele Smith

CARVED SOFTWOOD DOLL

With beads and applique textile dress, 14″ tall.

CUNA INDIAN, SAN BLAS ISLANDS,
PANAMA   20th C.

Collection of Martha W. Roth

PULL TOY   *following pages*

Carved wood. 20″ long.

GUATEMALA   20th C.

Collection of anonymous lender

PAINTED SCRAP WOOD TOY

7″ tall.

BRAZIL   20th C.

Collection of The Children's Museum, Indianapolis, Indiana

RED-DYED LEATHER HORSE

10″ tall.

BOLIVIA   20th C.

140   Collection of James Steele Smith

TOY YAK

Natural hair with glass eyes. 10″ tall.

NEPAL   c. 1984

Collection of anonymous lender

KNITTED WOOL DOLLS

10″ tall.

PERU   20th C.

Collection of The Children's Museum, Indianapolis, Indiana

CLOTH DOLLS WITH PAINTED FACES

12″ tall.

TURKEY, 20th C.

Collection of Mingei International

SHELL AND BEAD DOLL

Made over a bottle, with stopper head. 6″ tall.

ETHIOPIA   20th C.

Collection of Mingei International

MOVEABLE TOY

Carved wood. 4" tall.

U.S.S.R.   20th C.

Collection of The Children's Museum, Indianapolis, Indiana

PAINTED WOOD NESTING DOLLS

Lathe-turned, painted wood, 6" tall.

U.S.S.R.   20th C.

Collection of Mingei International and Bradley Smith

Bibliography

BARENHOLTZ, BERNARD AND McCLINTOCK, INEZ. *American Antique Toys.* New York: Harry N. Abrams, Inc., 1980.

FOX, CARL. *The Doll.* New York: Harry N. Abrams, Inc. (no date).

KETCHUM, WILLIAM C., JR. *Toys & Games.* Cooper-Hewitt Museum, Smithsonian Institution, 1981.

LONGENECKER, MARTHA, ed. *Folk Toys of the World.* Exhibition publication, Mingei International Museum of World Folk Art, San Diego, 1978.

MEIERS, FRED AND BARBARA *!vivan los artesanos!* Exhibition publication, Mingei International Museum of World Folk Art, San Diego, 1980.

MOOKERJEE, AJIT. *Folk Toys of India.* Calcutta & New Delhi: Oxford Book & Stationery Co., 1956.

NOBLE, JOHN. *Dolls.* New York: Walker and Company, 1967.

NOBLE, JOHN. *A Treasury of Beautiful Dolls.* New York: Hawthorn Books, Inc., 1971.

PETTIT, FLORENCE H. AND ROBERT M., *Mexican Folk Toys.* New York: Hastings House Publishers, 1978.

SAINT-GILLES, AMAURY. *Mingei.* Tokyo, 1983.

SHISHIDO, MISAKO. *The Folk Toys of Japan.* Tokyo: Japan Publications Trading Company, 1963.

SONOBE, KIYOSHI AND SAKAMOTO, KAZUYA. *Japanese Toys.* Tokyo, Japan and Rutland, Vermont: Bijutsu Shuppan-Sha and Charles E. Tuttle Company, Inc., 1965.

DALECARLIAN HORSE

Carved pine wood, 25″ tall.

SWEDEN

Collection of Sami Bandak

Lenders to the Exhibition

EVELYN ACKERMAN
SAMI BANDAK
JAMES & VARELEE BASSLER
KATHERINE BRADFORD
THE CHILDREN'S MUSEUM, INDIANAPOLIS, INDIANA
MARY H. CLARK
WILLIAM & MARION DENTZEL
DOROTHY DIXON
ANNE DOUGAL
BERNARD FINK
ERNEST & JEAN HAHN
LEANNE HINTON
MATT HINTON
SAM & LESLIE HINTON
KEITH & DONNA KAONIS
ELISABETH KIHLBERG
ALLYSON KNEIB
WINNIE LANGLEY
MARTHA LONGENECKER
ALTHEA D. LUCIC
FRED & BARBARA MEIERS
HARRY A. & JOYCE MILLER
MINGEI INTERNATIONAL MUSEUM
JOHN DARCY NOBLE
FRANK PAPWORTH
KATARINA REAL
ROBERTA SHAW
BRADLEY SMITH
JAMES STEELE SMITH
JOHN STANLEY
CONNIE STENGAL
CHIYO TELFORD
TOM TRAMEL
ANNE WEAVER
NANCY WILDERMUTH WEBBER
MARSHALL WISEMAN
BEATRICE WOOD

STRAW ANIMAL

With ribbon bands. 15″ tall.

Very similar toys are made in other European countries
such as Poland & Greece.

SCANDINAVIA

154   Collection of James Steele Smith

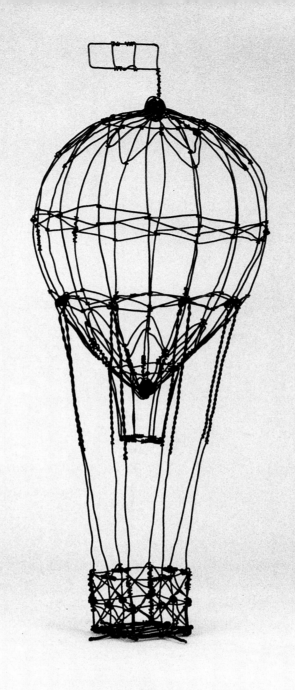

WIRE BALLOON
19″ tall.
MEXICO   1977

WIRE SHIP
President Mabubu's yacht by Lemere Alemi. 26″ long.
ZAIRE, AFRICA

156   Collection of The Children's Museum, Indianapolis, Indiana

MINGEI INTERNATIONAL MUSEUM

Board of Directors
ROGER C. CORNELL, M.D., President
MARTHA LONGENECKER, Vice President
DOROTHY STEWART, Vice President
JAMES F. MULVANEY, Secretary-Treasurer
KATY DESSENT
JEAN HAHN
ALTHEA D. LUCIC
MILLARD SHEETS, Honorary Board Member

International Advisory Board
LAURA ANDRESON, emeritus professor of art, U.C.L.A.
ELEANOR BEACH, American art lecturer & photographer
WARREN BEACH, former director of the Fine Arts Gallery of San Diego
RAND CASTILE, director of The Asian Art Museum, San Francisco
KATARINA REAL-CATE, anthropologist, South American folk art
KAMALADEVI CHATTOPADHYAYA, chairman emeritus of All India
　　Handicrafts Board
MRS. JOHN COLE, bibliographer of folk art
NORMAN COUSINS
ELIZABETH CUELLAR, curator of The Collection of International
　　Folk Art, The University of Mexico
THE HONORABLE & MRS. WARREN M. DORN
ROBERT BRUCE INVERARITY, museum director & consultant
JOHN NORTON, honorary consul of Sweden
JAMES S. PLAUT, art historian, cultural administrator
REAR ADMIRAL & MRS. W. HALEY ROGERS
TSUNE SESOKO, director, Cosmo Public Relations
HAKU SHAH, curator of the Tribal Research Museum, India
TATSUZO SHIMAOKA, one of Japan's foremost potters
THOMAS TIBBS, former director, La Jolla Museum of Contemporary
　　Art, lecturer in art, S.D.S.U.
LENNOX TIERNEY, professor, curator of Oriental art, University of Utah
SORI YANAGI, designer, son of founder of Mingei Association of Japan

MINGEI INTERNATIONAL IS A MEMBER OF COMBO

Legal Counsel　SHIRLEY KOVAR, Gary, Cary, Ames & Frye
C.P.A.　BRUCE HEAP, Hutchinson & Bloodgood, C.P.A.

Staff
MARTHA LONGENECKER, Director
NAN DANNINGER, Coordinator/Museum Program and
　　Manager of Collectors' Gallery
ROBERTA SHAW, Administrative Assistant/Development
TRISH BROWNING, Registrar
CYNTHIA CUADRA, Administrative Secretary
DOROTHEA CRONOGUE, Media Coordinator
JULIA BRASHARES, Secretary
ANNA SAULSBERY, Bookkeeper
BETTY GRENSTED, Librarian
FRANCES ARMSTRONG, Membership Co-Chairman
SUSAN EYER, Membership Co-Chairman
EILEEN MILLER, Volunteer Coordinator
PHYLLIS DOLE, Education Coordinator
ERIC SLOAN, Operations Assistant

Exhibition
JOHN DARCY NOBLE, Curatorial Consultant
MARTHA LONGENECKER, designer
JOANNE HEANEY, co-designer
STAFF & VOLUNTEER COUNCIL, installation
HUNTON SELLMAN, lighting
LINDA TEAGUE, floral arrangements
EILEEN MILLER, reception chairman

Publication
BRADLEY SMITH, Photography
MARTHA LONGENECKER--Design & Editing
MOOG & ASSOCIATES, INC., Typesetting
HELEN McCARTY, Production Assistant
DCS PACIFIC SERVICES, Color Separations and Printing

above
PULL TOY
By John Stanley. Carved painted wood. 6″ tall.
U.S.A.   Contemporary
Collection of John Stanley

Director's Circle

ERNEST W. AND JEAN E. HAHN, Honorary Chairmen
FRANCES ARMSTRONG
BARBARA BAEHR
ROSEMARIE BRAUN-UTECHT
DR. and MRS. ROBERT BUFFUM
SONDRA BUSCHMANN
MR. and MRS. J. DALLAS CLARK
ORA DeCONCINI
ROGER C. CORNELL, M.D.
DAVID COPLEY
MR. and MRS. ALEX DE BAKCSY
MR. and MRS. MICHAEL DESSENT
MR. and MRS. ROY DRACHMAN
MR. and MRS. EDWARD DRCAR
DR. and MRS. CHARLES EDWARDS
DR. and MRS. LAURENCE FAVROT
MR. and MRS. JOSEPH L. FRITZENKOTTER
MR. and MRS. JOHN E. GOODE
DR. and MRS. HUBERT GREENWAY
MR. and MRS. HERBERT HAIMSOHN
MR. and MRS. R.E. HAZARD
MR. and MRS. BRUCE M. HEAP
WILL HIPPEN, JR.
JOAN HOLTER
MR. and MRS. ROBERT INGOLD
LOUISA KASSLER
MR. and MRS. JAMES KERR
MR. and MRS. EUGENE KLEIN
MR. and MRS. WILLIAM KNEIB
DRS. MARY and ROBERT KNIGHT
DRS. VIRGINIA LIVINGSTON and OWEN WHEELER
MR. and MRS. FREDERICK T. MARSTON
MR. and MRS. JAMES F. MULVANEY
MR. JACK NAIMAN
DR. and MRS. KIRK PETERSON
DIANE POWERS, BAZAAR DEL MUNDO
MR. and MRS. GEORGE P. RODES
REAR ADMIRAL and MRS. W. HALEY ROGERS
SYDNEY MARTIN ROTH
ANNA M. SAULSBERY
MR. JOHN C. SCHUMACHER
MRS. JOHN SCHENEFIELD
MRS. THOMAS SHEPHERD
DR. BERNARD SIEGAN
MR. and MRS. WORLEY W. STEWART
MR. and MRS. JULES S. TRAUB
BARBARA WALBRIDGE
MR. and MRS. FRANK R. WARREN
LORI WINTER
MR. and MRS. WALTER ZABLE

Corporate Associates

The James S. Copley Foundation

MINGEI IS A TRANSCULTURAL WORD MEANING "ARTS OF THE PEOPLE." IT WAS COINED IN THE 1920's BY THE LATE DR. SOETSU YANAGI, REVERED SCHOLAR OF JAPAN, WHO COMBINED THE JAPANESE WORDS FOR PEOPLE (MIN) AND ART (GEI).

THESE ARE ESSENTIAL ARTS OF PEOPLE LIVING IN ALL TIMES THROUGHOUT THE WORLD WHICH SHARE IN COMMON A DIRECT SIMPLICITY AND JOY IN MAKING, BY HAND, ARTICLES BOTH USEFUL AND SATISFYING TO THE HUMAN SPIRIT.

MINGEI INTERNATIONAL, INCORPORATED IN 1974, IS A NON-PROFIT PUBLIC FOUNDATION DEDICATED TO FURTHERING THE UNDERSTANDING OF WORLD FOLK ARTS. ITS *MUSEUM OF WORLD FOLK ART* WAS ESTABLISHED MAY 5, 1978 AS A UNIQUE CENTER WHERE "ARTS OF THE PEOPLE" SPEAK DIRECTLY FOR THEMSELVES OF THE RICH DIVERSITY OF INDIVIDUALS AND CULTURES WHICH ARE THE ROOTS OF AMERICA. THROUGH THE UNIVERSAL LANGUAGE OF THE LINE, FORM, AND COLOR, THEY INSPIRE APPRECIATION OF THE SIMILARITIES AND DISTINCTIONS OF INDIVIDUALS AND CULTURES.

MINGEI INTERNATIONAL MUSEUM IS SUPPORTED BY MEMBERSHIPS, VOLUNTEER SERVICES, AND TAX-EXEMPT CONTRIBUTIONS (I.R.S. SECTION 501 c3). MEMBERSHIP IS OPEN TO THOSE WHO SHARE INTEREST IN THE MUSEUM'S DEDICATION.